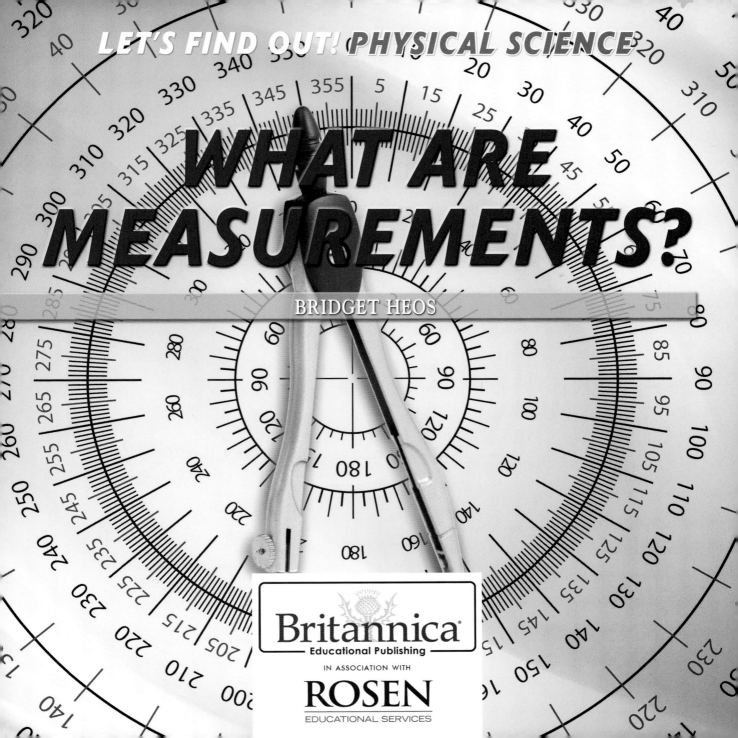

WHAT ARE MEASUREMENTS?

BRIDGET HEOS

Britannica
Educational Publishing

IN ASSOCIATION WITH

ROSEN
EDUCATIONAL SERVICES

Published in 2015 by Britannica Educational Publishing (a trademark of Encyclopædia Britannica, Inc.) in association with The Rosen Publishing Group, Inc.
29 East 21st Street, New York, NY 10010

Distributed exclusively by Rosen Publishing.
To see additional Britannica Educational Publishing titles, go to rosenpublishing.com.

First Edition

Britannica Educational Publishing
J.E. Luebering: Director, Core Reference Group
Mary Rose McCudden: Editor, Britannica Student Encyclopedia

Rosen Publishing
Hope Lourie Killcoyne: Executive Editor
Nelson Sá: Art Director
Nicole Russo: Designer
Cindy Reiman: Photography Manager
Amy Feinberg: Photo Researcher

Cataloging-in-Publication Data

Heos, Bridget, author.
What are measurements?/Bridget Heos. — First edition.
    pages cm — (Let's find out! Physical science)
Includes bibliographical references.
Audience: Grades 3-6.
ISBN 978-1-62275-507-3 (library bound) — ISBN 978-1-62275-509-7 (pbk.) — ISBN 978-1-62275-510-3 (6-pack)
1. Measurement—Juvenile literature. I. Title.
QA465.H467 2015
530.8—dc23

2014006026

Manufactured in the United States of America

Photo Credits
Cover, p. 1 (compass) oksana2010/Shutterstock.com; cover, p. 1, interior pages borders (protractor) Krall.Evelyn /Shutterstock.com, (background hues) Kotkoa/Shutterstock.com; p. 4 racorn/Shutterstock.com; p. 5 Lakhesis /iStock/Thinkstock; p. 6 rob3rt82/Shutterstock.com; p. 7 AFP/Getty Images; p. 8 Ryan McVay/Photodisc/Thinkstock; p. 9 Sarah Salmela/E+/Getty Images; p. 10 Matt Meadows/Photolibrary/Getty Images; p. 11 yalcinsonat1/iStock /Thinkstock; p. 12 IPGGutenbergUKLtd/iStock/Thinkstock; p. 13 CandyBox Images/Shutterstock.com; pp. 14, 29 Encyclopædia Britannica, Inc.; p. 15 Philippe Plailly/Science Source; p. 16 Ingram Publishing/Thinkstock; p. 17 Luciano Mortula/Shutterstock.com; p. 18 moodboard/Thinkstock; p. 19 FotografiaBasica/E+/Getty Images; p. 20 Matt Antonino/Shutterstock.com; p. 21 SafakOguz/iStock/Thinkstock; p. 22 Belinda Pretorius/Shutterstock.com; p. 23 Peter Muller/Cultura/Getty Images; p. 24 RusN/iStock/Thinkstock; p. 25 Willie B. Thomas/Vetta/Getty Images; p. 26 Magnascan/iStock/Thinkstock; p. 27 Sommai/Shutterstock.com; p. 28 Bernd Leitner/Getty Images.

CONTENTS

OVERVIEW

A measurement is the size, amount, or degree of an item. Many things can be measured, including length, area, volume, angles, weight, temperature, and time.

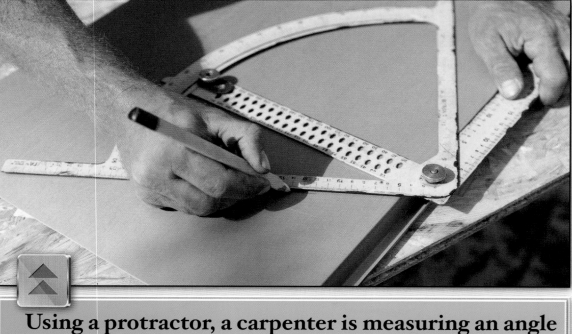

Using a protractor, a carpenter is measuring an angle so that he knows where to cut the board. Precise measurements are important in construction and many other fields.

Different measurements require different tools. For example, to measure the length of a piece of wood, you could use a ruler. But to measure temperature, you would use a thermometer. Different units are used, too. Length can be measured in meters (in the metric system) or feet (in the English system). There are also smaller and larger units. The important thing is that each unit always represents the same standard.

A **unit** is a definite quantity used as a standard of measurement.

A thermometer measures temperature. As you can see, this thermometer is measuring something very cold. How many degrees below zero is it showing?

STANDARD MEASUREMENTS

In order to be accurate, all measurements must make a comparison with something called a standard. A standard is an amount upon which everyone agrees. Units are the names for different standards. For example, one unit for weight is the gram. Everyone agrees that 1 gram is a certain amount of weight. Two grams equal twice that amount, and so on.

Some standards are based on fundamental laws of nature. For instance, the meter is defined as the distance traveled by

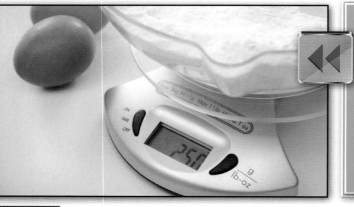

One gram means the same thing everywhere. That way, when people bake cakes, they always use the right amount of sugar.

light in a vacuum during a period of 1/299,792,458th of a second. Other standards are physical items. For example, the kilogram is measured as being equal to the mass of an actual metal cylinder. This cylinder is housed in France and is known as the "international prototype kilogram."

THINK ABOUT IT

What if there were no standard measurements? If you and somebody else both measured the length of a room with your feet, for instance, what problem might arise?

The original kilogram standard is kept under glass at the International Bureau of Weights and Measures in France. It is made of platinum and iridium.

THE ENGLISH SYSTEM

Throughout history, people have come up with many systems of measurement. The two most widely used are the English system and the metric system. In the English system, the inch is a unit of length. There are 12 inches in 1 foot and 5,280 feet in 1 mile. The cup is a unit of volume. There are 2

A gallon (as in a gallon of milk or orange juice) is a unit in the English system. In the United States, drinks are sold in both liters (metric) and gallons (English).

The unit "foot" is named for the fact that people used to measure short distances with their feet. What other units are named for everyday objects?

cups in 1 pint, 2 pints in 1 quart, and 4 quarts in 1 gallon. The ounce is the unit of weight. There are 16 ounces in a pound and 2,000 pounds in a ton.

Many unit names come from everyday objects used to measure things hundreds of years ago. The length of a person's foot was used to measure short distances, for example, and a household cup was used to measure liquids. Eventually people set standards. The English system became the first worldwide system of measurement.

THINK ABOUT IT
How many cups are in a gallon?

THE METRIC SYSTEM

In the metric system, the meter is the basic unit of length, the liter is the unit of volume, and the gram is the unit of weight. Each unit is divided into smaller units or combined into larger units by multiples of 10.

Three of these items contain 1 liter of liquid. The cube is 1,000 cubic centimeters, which is equivalent to one liter.

"Centi" means "1/100." One centimeter is 1/100 of a meter. How many centimeters are on a ruler that is 1 meter long?

Standard prefixes are added to the basic unit to tell how many multiples of 10 are in a unit. For example, "kilo" means "thousand," so there are 1,000 meters in 1 kilometer. The prefix "centi" means "1/100," so 1 centimeter is 1/100 of a meter.

COMPARE AND CONTRAST

In the metric system, 1 kilogram equals 1,000 grams. In the English system, 1 pound equals 16 ounces. Compare and contrast larger and smaller units in the metric and English systems.

Two Systems

France adopted the metric system in 1795. Soon after, the U.S. Congress considered adopting it. But people were more familiar with the English system, so Americans continued to use it instead. By the mid-1900s, most countries had adopted the metric system exclusively.

In the United States, the metric system is used in the science, medical, engineering, automobile, electronics, electrical, and manufacturing fields. However, the United States has not adopted the system exclusively. The

The metric system is the only measurement system used in many countries. In the United States, it is used by scientists, engineers, and many others.

English system can still be seen on road signs (miles, not kilometers, per hour), in cookbooks (cups, not milliliters), and in many construction projects (inches, not centimeters). To prepare students for jobs that require knowledge of the metric and English systems, schools teach both.

THINK ABOUT IT
In track and field, four laps around the track measure 1 mile, or 1,609 meters. What is the distance of one lap around the track in meters?

Cookbooks published outside of the United States use grams and milliliters, not teaspoons and cups. Many online recipes offer both options.

MEASURING DISTANCE

Distance is the amount of space between two points. A ruler can be used to measure short distances. On a metric ruler, a millimeter is the smallest unit. There are 10 millimeters in a centimeter. On an English system ruler, inches are commonly divided into sixteenths of an inch.

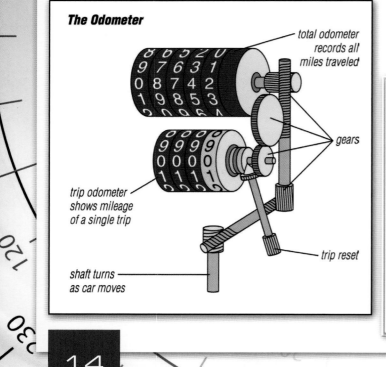

The Odometer

total odometer records all miles traveled

gears

trip odometer shows mileage of a single trip

trip reset

shaft turns as car moves

An odometer works by counting the revolutions (turns) of a wheel. That number, multiplied by the circumference of the tire on the wheel, is the distance traveled.

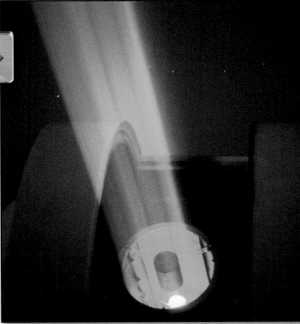

Lasers can measure very long distances. This laser is being used to measure the distance between Earth and the Moon.

For longer distances, an odometer can be used. In a car or bicycle, an odometer measures distance by counting the number of revolutions (turns) of a wheel. With each revolution, the wheel travels a certain distance forward. Very long distances can be measured with lasers. A light beam is emitted from a laser and reflected back to the source. The travel time of the beam is measured. Because the speed of light is known, the distance can be found.

A laser is a device that uses the natural vibrations of atoms or molecules to generate a narrow beam of light.

MEASURING PERIMETER AND AREA

To build a fence around a garden, would you need to know the area or the perimeter of the garden?

Distance refers to a line, which has only length. A rectangular region on a flat surface has length and width. The perimeter is the distance around that region. To build a fence around a garden, you would measure each side of the garden and then add them up. The length of the fence would equal the sum of the length of the garden's four sides (its perimeter).

Area is the amount of space within a region. It is measured in square units. Imagine laying 1-foot-square tiles on a patio so that they didn't overlap and there was no empty space. The number of tiles used would be the number of square feet, or area, of the patio. Area is calculated by multiplying length by width.

To tile the patio next to your garden, would you need to know the area or the perimeter of the patio?

THINK ABOUT IT
Find the perimeter and area of a square with 10-foot sides.

MEASURING VOLUME

A solid object has length, width, and height. Volume is the amount of space within the object. To determine the volume of a box, you would measure its height,

To find the volume of this box, the man needs to measure its height, width, and length, and multiply the three measurements.

width, and length, and multiply these three things. For instance, the volume of a box with 10-foot sides would be 10 × 10 × 10, or 1,000 **cubic** feet.

To visualize what a cubic unit is, imagine filling the box with smaller boxes, each with 1-foot sides. The number of boxes that would fit without empty space would be the number of cubic feet.

Cubic means having length, width, and height.

To measure the volume of this box, you could count how many smaller boxes, known as cubic units, fit inside.

Measuring Round Objects

Of course, not all items have straight sides. Circular objects are measured by finding their diameter, which is the distance across the center of the circle. Then a special number known as pi, approximately 3.1416, is used. The circumference, or perimeter, of a circle is calculated by multiplying

You can measure the area of a pie with the help of pi, a special number that is approximately 3.1416.

the diameter by pi. So the circumference of a circle with a 10-foot diameter would be approximately 31.4 feet.

The radius (appearing as "r" in formulas) is half the diameter. The area of the same circle would be found by multiplying pi times the radius squared (radius squared is r × r). So the circle discussed here would have an area of about 78.5 square feet. The same figures can be used to calculate the volume of a cylinder (pi × r squared × length).

A pipe is a cylinder. To measure the volume of a cylinder, you must know its radius and length. You must also use pi.

COMPARE AND CONTRAST
How much greater is the area of a 10-foot square than the area of a circle with a 10-foot diameter?

Measuring Weight

Technically, weight describes the effect of gravity on an object. But most people think of weight as the heaviness of something. In the metric system, weight is measured in grams. One thousand milligrams equal 1 gram. One thousand grams equal 1 kilogram. One thousand kilograms equal 1 metric ton. In the English system, the unit for weight is a pound. There are 16 ounces in 1 pound and 2,000 pounds in 1 ton

Balance scales like this one have been used since ancient times. Known weights are placed on one side and the items being measured on the other side.

At home, a scale might be off by a pound or two. In science, precise measurements are essential, and scales must be accurate.

(which is different from a metric ton). Weight is measured using a scale. Since ancient times, balance scales have been used. A known weight and the item being weighed are placed on either side of a beam balanced on a fulcrum. When the sides are balanced, it means that the item being weighed equals the known weight. Today, electronic scales are commonly used.

A **fulcrum** is the support on which a lever rests.

MEASURING ANGLES

An angle is the space between two lines that meet at a point. Angles are measured in degrees. A protractor is the tool used to measure angles. It forms one or two half circles, which each total 180 degrees. Laying the baseline flat against

Degrees can be measured with a protractor. There are 360 degrees in a circle.

one line, the other line points to the number of degrees in the angle. A 180-degree angle is known as a straight angle. It looks like a straight line. A 90-degree angle is known as a right angle. One line lies flat, and the other points straight up.

A **degree** is a unit of measure for angles. It equals 1/360 of the circumference of a circle.

An angle in between a right angle and straight angle (between 90 and 180 degrees) is called an obtuse angle. An angle that is less than 90 degrees is an acute angle.

MEASURING TEMPERATURE

Temperature is the hotness or coolness of something. The metric unit of temperature is a degree Celsius, or degree C. The freezing point of water is 0 degrees C. The boiling point is 100 degrees C. In the United States, the Fahrenheit degree is a common unit. The freezing point of water is 32 degrees F, and 212 degrees is the boiling point.

Another unit, the kelvin (K), does not include the term "degree." A single kelvin

It is easy to remember the boiling point of water in the metric system. It is 100 degrees Celsius.

equals a single degree C. However, 0 K is much colder than 0 degrees C.

The freezing point of water in the metric system is 0 degrees C. Here's another handy number to remember: 20 degrees C could be the temperature on a beautiful spring day.

THINK ABOUT IT
To convert Fahrenheit to Celsius, the formula is (degrees F − 32) ÷ 1.8. Based on this equation, convert 70 degrees F to degrees C.

MEASURING TIME

Time is the progress of events in the past, present, and future. The same units of time are used in the English system and metric system. Unlike most metric units, units of time are not based on 10. There are 60 seconds in a minute, 60 minutes in an hour, 24 hours in a day, and 365 ¼ days in a year. Seconds, however, are divided into tenths, hundredths, thousandths, etc.

Time is measured by clocks. Atomic clocks are among the most

The time of day is measured in hours, minutes, and seconds. Digital clocks are common today. Can you tell what time it is on the analog watch?

accurate. For these clocks, the second is based on the number of vibrations of a certain kind of atom. International time is set according to the average time of several atomic clocks.

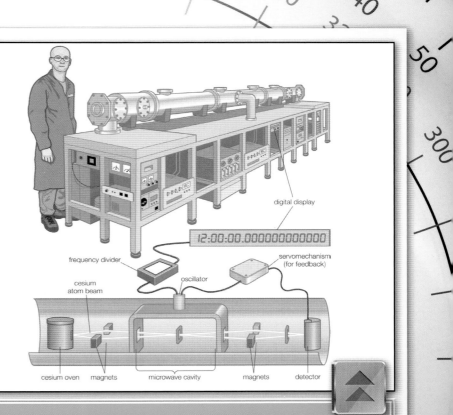

digital display

12:00:00.000000000000

frequency divider

servomechanism
(for feedback)

cesium
atom beam

oscillator

cesium oven   magnets   microwave cavity   magnets   detector

We tell time by looking at a clock. But how do our clocks know what time it is? They are set with the help of atomic clocks like this one.

Think About It

What would a clock based on the number 10 look like? For instance, there might be 100 minutes in an hour. But how many seconds would each minute have in a 100-minute hour?

GLOSSARY

angles Figures formed by two lines extending from the same point.

area The surface inside a figure or shape.

circumference The perimeter of a circle.

distance The space between two points, lines, surfaces, or objects.

English system A system of weights and measures in which the foot is the principal unit of length and the pound is the principal unit of weight.

length The measurement of the long or longer side of something; any measured distance.

measurement The act or process of determining the extent or amount of an item.

metric system A system of weights and measures based on the meter and on the kilogram.

pi The ratio of the circumference of a circle to its diameter. Its value is approximately 3.1416.

scale A tool used for weighing.

standard Something set up by authority or by general consent as a basis for measuring.

temperature The degree of hotness or coldness of something, as shown by a thermometer.

time The period during which an action, process, or condition exists or continues.

volume An amount of space as measured in cubic units.

weight The heaviness of an object; scientifically, the effect of gravity on an object.

width The measurement of the short or shorter side of something.

For More Information

Books

Adler, David, and Edward Miller. *Perimeter, Area, and Volume: A Monster Book of Dimensions*. New York, NY: Holiday House, 2013.

Basher, Simon, and Dan Green. *Math: A Book You Can Count On*. New York, NY: Kingfisher, 2010.

Farrell, Karen, Cathy Weiskopf, Linda Powley, and Tom Kerr. *Estimating and Measuring* (Adventures in Mathopolis). Hauppauge, NY: Barron's Educational, 2008.

Irving, Dianne. *Perimeter and Area at the Amusement Park*. Mankato, MN: Capstone, 2011.

Somervill, Barbara. *Mass and Weight* (A+ Books: Measure It!). Portsmouth, NH: Heinemann, 2010.

Websites

Because of the changing nature of Internet links, Rosen Publishing has developed an online list of websites related to the subject of this book. This site is updated regularly. Please use this link to access the list:

http://www.rosenlinks.com/lfo/meas

INDEX